D1518804

KANSAS CITY
CHIEFS

by Brian Lester

Published by ABDO Publishing Company, 8000 West 78th Street, Edina, Minnesota 55439. Copyright © 2011 by Abdo Consulting Group, Inc. International copyrights reserved in all countries. No part of this book may be reproduced in any form without written permission from the publisher. SportsZone™ is a trademark and logo of ABDO Publishing Company.

Printed in the United States of America,
North Mankato, Minnesota
062010
092010

 THIS BOOK CONTAINS AT LEAST 10% RECYCLED MATERIALS.

Editor: Chrös McDougall
Copy Editor: Nicholas Cafarelli
Interior Design and Production: Christa Schneider
Cover Design: Craig Hinton

Photo Credits: David Drapkin/AP Images, cover; AP Images, title page, 7, 9, 17, 25, 42 (bottom); NFL Photos/AP Images, 4, 12, 18, 26, 29, 31, 37, 42 (middle), 43 (top); Paul Spinelli/AP Images, 10, 39, 43 (bottom); Carl Linde/AP Images, 15, 42 (top); Rich Clarkson/AP Images, 20, 23; David Stluka/AP Images, 33, 34, 43 (middle); Kevin Terrell/AP Images, 41; Charlie Riedel/AP Images, 44; Julia Robertson/AP Images, 47

Library of Congress Cataloging-in-Publication Data
Lester, Brian, 1975-
  Kansas City Chiefs / Brian Lester.
      p. cm. — (Inside the NFL)
  ISBN 978-1-61714-016-7
  1. Kansas City Chiefs (Football team)—History—Juvenile literature. I. Title.
  GV956.K35L47 2010
  796.332'6409778411—dc22
                        2010017022

TABLE OF CONTENTS

CHAPTER 1

A NEW BEGINNING

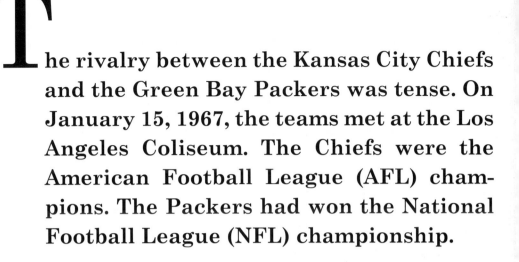

T

he rivalry between the Kansas City Chiefs and the Green Bay Packers was tense. On January 15, 1967, the teams met at the Los Angeles Coliseum. The Chiefs were the American Football League (AFL) champions. The Packers had won the National Football League (NFL) championship.

This was the first AFL-NFL World Championship Game. It would later become known as Super Bowl I.

Each team was playing for the pride of its league. The NFL and AFL had agreed one year earlier to have their champions play each other. Each league wanted to show that it was the stronger one. Coming into the game, most people thought the NFL was the superior league.

The Chiefs fought hard to change that opinion. They had slowed the Packers' famed running attack in the first half. They had also made the Packers legendary quarterback Bart Starr look simply ordinary.

QUARTERBACK LEN DAWSON LED THE AFL-CHAMPION CHIEFS TO THE FIRST-EVER SUPER BOWL IN 1967 AGAINST THE GREEN BAY PACKERS.

SUPER BOWL I

The first Super Bowl was much different from what we are used to today. In fact, it was not even called the Super Bowl at the time. It as known as the AFL-NFL World Championship Game. It would be labeled as Super Bowl I at a later date.

The changes started with the coin toss. Instead of calling on an NFL great to toss the coin, the game officials handled the duties. The game did not have a flashy music star perform a halftime show, either. Instead, the bands from the University of Arizona and the University of Michigan performed.

The fan experience was much different, as well. Unlike today, the stadium was not even sold out. Tickets for the first Super Bowl cost $12. Today, a fan hoping to attend the NFL's biggest came has to be willing to drop at least $500 for a ticket. Some ticket brokers charge thousands of dollars for top seats at the game.

Green Bay had opened the scoring. They took a 7–0 lead on a touchdown pass by Starr. But the Chiefs soon answered. In the second quarter, Chiefs quarterback Len Dawson marched his team down the field. On the sixth play of the drive, Dawson was forced to scramble. But he found receiver Curtis McClinton for a 7-yard touchdown pass.

At halftime, the Packers' lead was only 14–10. The Chiefs and their coach, Hank Stram, could sense an upset. So could the 63,036 fans in attendance. But it was not to be.

The Chiefs' momentum would fade early in the second half. Dawson had moved the Chiefs to their own 49-yard line. On the next play, the Packers blitzed. Dawson struggled under the pressure.

KANSAS CITY RUNNING BACK MIKE GARRETT CARRIES THE BALL AGAINST THE GREEN BAY PACKERS IN SUPER BOWL I IN 1967.

He tried to fire a pass, but it was tipped. The ball wobbled through the air before landing in the hands of Packers defensive back Willie Wood. He then

DID YOU KNOW?

Chiefs' owner Lamar Hunt would later coin the term Super Bowl. *He came up with the name after watching his daughter play with a toy called a Super Ball.*

returned it to the Chiefs' 5-yard line. The Packers scored a touchdown on the next play.

Green Bay never looked back. They scored 21 unanswered points in a 35–10 win over the Chiefs.

Kansas City defensive tackle Jerry Mays was quick to credit the Packers for their victory. But he did not think the Chiefs were as bad as the final score indicated.

SUPER STRAM

Hank Stram was considered a great talent evaluator. That showed during his time with the Chiefs. Five of the Kansas City players he coached are now in the Hall of Fame. Stram's head coaching career began in 1960 with the Dallas Texans. In 1963, the Texans moved to Kansas City and became the Chiefs. Stram coached the Texans and Chiefs for 15 years. During that time he became the only coach in AFL history to take his team to two Super Bowls. He also had a league-best three AFL championships. Stram was inducted into the Pro Football Hall of Fame in 2003.

"We had to stop Green Bay on those third-and-one and -two plays," Mays said. "Then they killed us on third-and-six and third-and-long. The way I see it, we lost our poise after Wood's interception. The Packers themselves beat us in the first half, then the Packers and the Packer myth beat us in the second."

Chiefs defensive tackle Buck Buchanan did not believe the Chiefs were that much worse than the Packers, either. He was eager for a rematch as soon as the final whistle blew.

"I'd like to play them again next year, or next week, or even tomorrow," Buchanan said.

Kansas City would return to Super Bowl IV in 1970. It was their second trip in ten years as a pro football franchise. The Chiefs' second try turned out better than the first. Kansas

CHIEFS COACH HANK STRAM IS CARRIED AWAY IN CELEBRATION AFTER HIS TEAM DEFEATED THE MINNESOTA VIKINGS IN SUPER BOWL IV.

City beat the Minnesota Vikings 23–7.

After Super Bowl IV, the AFL and NFL officially merged to become one league. The Chiefs would go on to have many thrilling moments after joining the NFL. But they are still waiting to match their glory days from Super Bowls I and IV.

CHAPTER 2

THE EARLY YEARS

Lamar Hunt dreamed of owning a pro football team. He was in his twenties when he first tried to get an NFL team in Dallas, Texas. But every time he applied for a team, the league rejected him. These repeated rejections frustrated Hunt. In 1959, when he was 26 years old, Hunt tried something else.

Hunt approached other potential owners about creating their own professional football league. Seven months later, they had created the AFL. Hunt was one of eight original owners.

The team owners met on August 14, 1959, at a hotel in Chicago, Illinois. There, they discussed the start of the league. Hunt's team would play in his hometown and be called the Dallas Texans. The other teams would be the Boston Patriots, Buffalo Bills, Denver Broncos, Houston Oilers, Los Angeles Chargers, New York Titans, and a Minneapolis, Minnesota, team. However, the Minneapolis team dropped out

LAMAR HUNT, SHOWN IN 2006, HELPED ESTABLISH THE DALLAS TEXANS AND THE AMERICAN FOOTBALL LEAGUE IN 1959.

CURTIS MCCLINTON (32) AND LEN DAWSON (16) POSE WITH AFL COMMISSIONER JOE FOSS AFTER THE 1962 AFL CHAMPIONSHIP WIN.

to join the NFL before the first season. The team that would become known as the Oakland Raiders replaced them.

Few people believed the AFL could survive. But after six seasons, the league was still growing. So much, in fact, that the NFL decided it was better to merge leagues than compete.

The AFL and NFL Champions began playing each other after the 1966 season. The two leagues merged into one for the 1970 season. Hunt was a large reason for the AFL's success.

"Before there was a player, coach or a general manager in the league, there was Lamar Hunt," former Boston Patriots owner William Sullivan said at Hunt's induction into the Pro Football Hall of Fame in 1972. "Hunt was the cornerstone, the integrity of the league. Without him, there would have been no AFL."

The Dallas Texans played in the Cotton Bowl Stadium. Although they competed with the NFL's Dallas Cowboys, the Texans had strong local support. The team averaged 24,500 fans per game in its first season. It was the highest attendance in the league.

Part of the Texans' appeal was that they featured several former college stars from the state. Quarterback Cotton Davidson played at Baylor University in Waco. Fullback Jack Spikes was from Texas Christian University near Dallas. Running back Abner Haynes was from North Texas State.

On September 10, 1960, the Texans went to Los Angeles to play the Chargers. It was their first game in the new league. The Texans jumped out to an early lead on a 12-yard touchdown pass from Davidson to Chris Burford. A 1-yard touchdown run by Jack Spikes gave Dallas a 13–0 lead.

The Chargers came back with a touchdown. But Haynes caught a 17-yard touchdown pass from Davidson to put the Texans ahead 20–7 at halftime.

MR. FRANCHISE

Between 1960 and 1962, Abner Haynes scored 44 touchdowns and tallied more than 4,000 yards of total offense. He was named the AFL's first rookie of the year. He was also named the league's first Most Valuable Player that year. Texans head coach Hank Stram called Haynes a "franchise player."

"He was a franchise player before they talked about franchise players," Stram said. "He did it all—rushing, receiving, kickoff returns, punt returns."

An opening-day victory seemed to be in the works. But the second half did not go as planned for the Texans. They were held scoreless. Los Angeles ended up winning 21–20.

The Texans had much better luck the following week in Oakland. Davidson threw two touchdown passes. Spikes also kicked two field goals and ran for a touchdown. The Texans blasted the Oakland Raiders 34–16 for their first win.

Dallas had a powerful offense. They scored 30 or more points six times that season. But the Texans failed to contend for a Western Division title. They finished 8–6. Haynes finished the year with a league-high 875 rushing yards and nine touchdowns. His performance earned him player of the year honors in the AFL's first season.

The Texans struggled in their second season, finishing 6–8. Their fall was fueled by a seven-game losing streak during the middle of the season.

The 1962 season seemed to have a special feel for Texans fans. The team brought in Len Dawson. The quarterback had spent six seasons in the NFL but had yet to become a star. They also signed Curtis McClinton, a rookie fullback who had a lot of potential.

The Texans plowed through the competition. They finished 11–3 and won the Western Division championship.

Dawson threw for more than 2,700 yards and 29 touchdowns that season. Dallas also had the league's highest-scoring offense. The dynamic backfield of Haynes and McClinton gave opponents headaches. Haynes

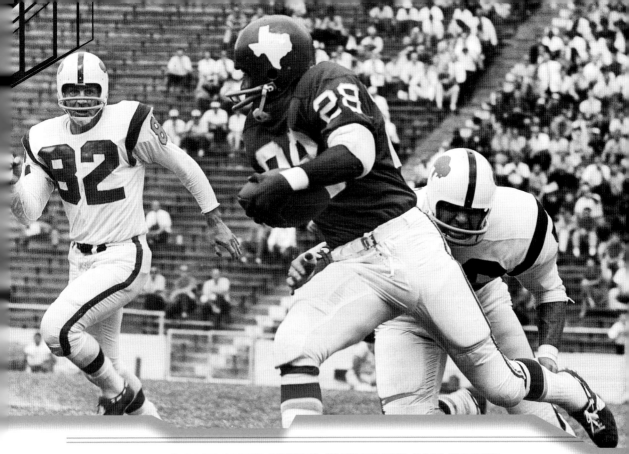

TEXANS RUNNING BACK ABNER HAYNES CARRIES THE BALL UPFIELD AGAINST THE BILLS IN 1962.

ran for 1,049 yards and 13 touchdowns while McClinton had 604 rushing yards and two touchdowns.

Dallas faced the in-state rival Houston Oilers in the AFL Championship Game. The Oilers had won the AFL's first two titles. They were heavily favored against the Texans on a cloudy and wet afternoon at Jeppesen Stadium in Houston. An energized crowd of 37,981 filled the stadium. A national television audience tuned in as well.

Dallas dominated the first half. It charged out to a 17–0 lead. But the defending AFL champions tied the game at 17–17. The Texans were on the brink of defeat with only three minutes left in the game.

Houston's George Blanda lined up for a field goal from the 42-yard line. After the snap, Texans linebacker Sherrill Headrick burst through the offensive line. He reached up and got his hand on the ball to block the kick. The game headed to overtime.

A coin flip determined who got the ball first. Dallas won the coin toss. But Haynes decided to kick off against the wind.

ON TARGET

Len Dawson was known for being calm and cool under pressure. Because he was rarely nervous, Dawson was an accurate passer. Dawson was the top passer in the AFL four times (1962, 1964, 1966, 1968). During his career, he threw for more than 28,000 yards and tossed 239 touchdown passes. His coach, Hank Stram, said Dawson was "the most accurate passer in the NFL."

"The players were excited and tugging at Abner," Texans coach Hank Stram said. "He just didn't understand the option. It was a mistake you don't like to make."

The mistake did not cost the Texans the game. Neither team scored during the first 15-minute overtime period. Then, Dallas kicker Tommy Brooker made a game-winning 25-yard field goal less than three minutes into the second overtime. Dallas won the game 20–17.

That AFL title would be the final highlight for the Texans. Despite their success, the team had trouble convincing fans they were at the same level as the NFL's Cowboys. Hunt decided to move the team to Kansas City before the 1963 season.

TEAMMATES CARRY TEXANS KICKER TOMMY BROOKER AFTER HE KICKED THE GAME-WINNING FIELD GOAL IN THE 1962 AFL CHAMPIONSHIP GAME.

CHAPTER 3

GOING TO KANSAS CITY

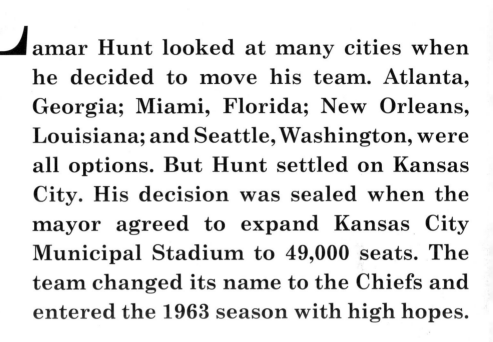

L amar Hunt looked at many cities when he decided to move his team. Atlanta, Georgia; Miami, Florida; New Orleans, Louisiana; and Seattle, Washington, were all options. But Hunt settled on Kansas City. His decision was sealed when the mayor agreed to expand Kansas City Municipal Stadium to 49,000 seats. The team changed its name to the Chiefs and entered the 1963 season with high hopes.

The 1963 AFL Draft had been a good one for the Chiefs. Kansas City drafted defensive tackle Buck Buchanan, guard Ed Budde, and linebacker Bobby Bell. The three combined to play in 526 games with the Chiefs.

But there was also tragedy for the Chiefs before the season started. Stone Johnson was a rookie running back with a lot of potential. But he broke his neck in a preseason game. Johnson died 10 days later.

GUARD ED BUDDE LINES UP BEFORE THE SNAP AGAINST THE VIKINGS IN SUPER BOWL IV. BUDDE WAS A SEVEN-TIME PRO BOWL SELECTION.

KANSAS CITY CORNERBACK DAVE GRAYSON TACKLES A DENVER BRONCOS PLAYER AT KANSAS CITY MUNICIPAL STADIUM IN 1963.

The Chiefs opened their first season in Kansas City with a 59–7 win over the Denver Broncos. The victory was one of the few highlights during a difficult season. The Chiefs finished 5–7–2.

The 1964 season was not much better. With injuries to several key players, the Chiefs finished 7–7. An average of only 18,126 fans came to their home games. The other AFL owners became concerned about the Chiefs' future in Kansas City.

The Chiefs stayed in Kansas City. But their luck did not improve in 1965. They had drafted future Hall of Fame running back Gale Sayers from the

University of Kansas. But the Chiefs lost him in a bidding war with the NFL's Chicago Bears.

The team also had to deal with another tragedy. Running back Mack Lee Hill died while undergoing routine knee surgery that December. The cause of his death was a sudden and massive pulmonary embolism, a blockage in a lung artery.

On the field, Kansas City lost two games by a field goal or less. They finished the year 7–5–2. But the luck of the Chiefs would change in 1966. Kansas City won its first three games on the road and returned home for a showdown against the defending AFL champion Buffalo Bills.

A record crowd of 43,885 filled Municipal Stadium to watch the Chiefs battle the Bills. The fans had a lot to smile about early on. Dawson threw a 71-yard touchdown pass to Otis Taylor to give the Chiefs a 7–0 lead. The Chiefs led 14–6 after one quarter. But the Bills fought back. Buffalo left town with a 29–14 victory.

The loss did not rattle the confidence of the Chiefs, though. They went on to finish 11–2–1. They also won the Western Division by three games. The strong finish set up another showdown between the Chiefs and Bills in the AFL Championship Game.

MAKING A MARK

Willie Lanier was the first African-American pro football player to play middle linebacker. He spent 11 seasons with the Kansas City Chiefs. Lanier was one of the most feared defensive players in football. He earned the nickname "Contact" because of the powerful hits he put on opposing players. But Lanier was also known for making interceptions. Except for the first and last seasons of his career, he intercepted at least two passes every season. He also recovered 18 fumbles during his career.

WISHFUL THINKING

Kansas City qualified for Super Bowl I before their opponent. Some of the players were hoping for a game against the Green Bay Packers.

"The reason I'd rather play Green Bay is that the Packers are established as the best in the NFL over a period of years," All-AFL defensive end and tackle Jerry Mays said. "We want to play the best. If we had to play Dallas and we beat the Cowboys, people would say 'Oh well, the Cowboys were a fluke team, anyway."

Most football fans figured the Chiefs would be no match for the Packers. But the Chiefs hung in there for a half. Kansas City trailed only 14–10 at halftime. But the Packers ultimately dominated the second half and won 35–10.

The Chiefs were confident heading into War Memorial Stadium in Buffalo. Dawson shined on the cold and wet December afternoon in western New York. He completed 16 of 24 passes for 227 yards and a touchdown. The Chiefs won 31–7.

"This," Dawson said, "is the second most thrilling day of my life. The first most thrilling is coming up on January 15." That date might not have been as memorable as Dawson would have hoped. The Chiefs lost to the Packers in Super Bowl I.

The Chiefs had an uphill battle in the 1967 season trying to repeat as AFL champions. Kansas City finished 9–5 in an injury-filled season. But they bounced back in 1968. The Chiefs finished 12–2 and tied the Oakland Raiders for first

CHIEFS RUNNING BACK WARREN MCVEA LOOKS FOR SPACE AGAINST THE HOUSTON OILERS IN 1969.

place in the Western Division. The tie set up a playoff game between the Chiefs and Raiders. However, the Chiefs lost 41–6.

The 1969 AFL season was the last before the league merged with the NFL. The Chiefs overcame an injury to Dawson to finish 11–3. They were second in the Western Division. But because the AFL added another playoff round, the Chiefs were headed to the postseason.

First they faced quarterback Joe Namath and the New York Jets. Kansas City's stubborn defense gave the defending Super Bowl champions no breaks in a 13–6 victory.

The Chiefs then headed to Oakland for an AFL Championship Game against the Raiders.

With the score tied 7–7 at half-time, Stram gave a motivational speech to his players. "'Turn it on,' I told them. 'Give it all you've got. It's in our grasp, now squeeze it,'" Stram said.

The Chiefs came out and knocked off the Raiders 17–7. They were heading to Super Bowl IV. There, the Chiefs met the NFL's Minnesota Vikings. The Chiefs players took pride in representing the AFL in Super Bowl IV. The players even wore "A-10" patches that symbolized the 10 years the AFL had been in existence. But the odds were against the Chiefs. The Vikings were known for their tough defense. They were favored to win by at least 12 points.

A record crowd of more than 80,000 fans showed up for the game. The Chiefs went after the Vikings early. Running back Mike Garrett scored a touchdown and Jan Stenerud kicked three field goals. The Chiefs built a 16–0 halftime lead.

Dawson played at his best, too. He completed 12 of his 17 passes. His highlight was a 46-yard touchdown pass to Otis Taylor. That sealed a 23–7 win over the Vikings.

The AFL era had ended on a high note. The league had proved it was for real and was ready for the merger with the NFL.

HALL OF FAME KICKER

Jan Stenerud was the first true place-kicker to be inducted into the Pro Football Hall of Fame. He was inducted in 1992. During his 19-year career, Stenerud scored 1,699 points and made 373 field goals.

WILLIE LANIER WAS A DOMINANT FORCE AT MIDDLE LINEBACKER. HE PLAYED 11 SEASONS, ALL WITH KANSAS CITY.

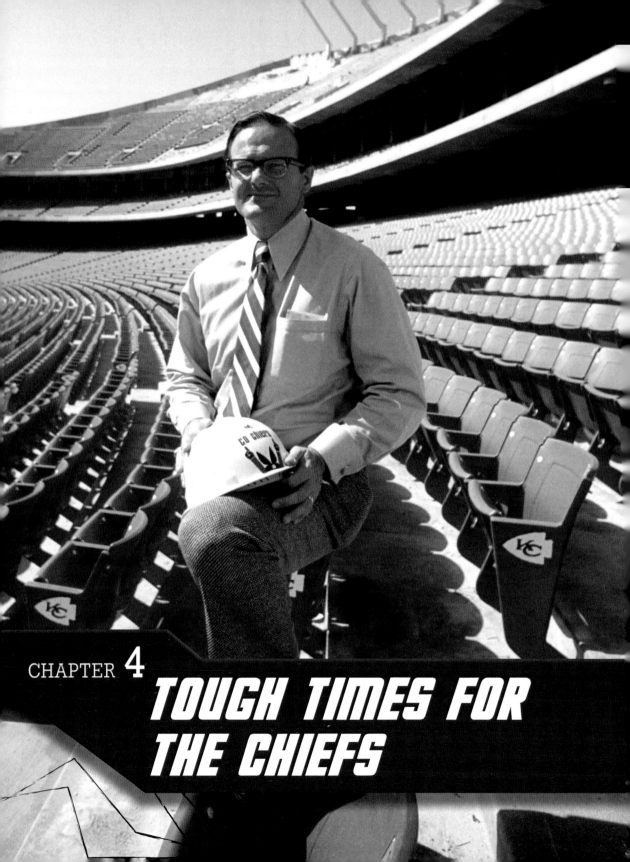

CHAPTER 4

TOUGH TIMES FOR THE CHIEFS

Kansas City was unable to build on the success from its Super Bowl win. The Chiefs missed the playoffs in 1970. They bounced back in 1971. Kicker Jan Stenerud nailed a field goal to give the Chiefs a late-season 16–14 win over the Oakland Raiders to clinch the Western Division title.

The Chiefs faced the Miami Dolphins in the first round of the playoffs on Christmas Day. It was also the final game at Municipal Stadium in Kansas City. But it was not a memorable exit for Chiefs fans. Stenerud missed a field goal attempt with 35 seconds left in the fourth quarter. He had another game-winning try blocked in overtime. The Chiefs lost 27–24 in double overtime.

AMAZING EFFORT

Ed Podolak had one of his best performances during the Christmas Day playoff game against the Dolphins. He carried the ball 17 times for 85 yards, caught eight passes for 110 yards, and rolled up 153 yards on kickoff returns.

CHIEFS OWNER LAMAR HUNT POSES IN THE TEAM'S ARROWHEAD STADIUM, WHICH OPENED IN 1972.

A TRUE HERO

Joe Delaney did not know how to swim very well. But when the Chiefs' running back saw three children drowning in a hole filled with water during the summer of 1983, he did not hesitate. He immediately jumped in to try to save them. He did everything he could to rescue them. But two of the three boys drowned. Delaney also drowned on that June afternoon in Louisiana.

Delaney had a lot of potential as an NFL player. He had been an All-American in 1979 and 1980 at Northwestern State University. The Chiefs selected him in the second round of the 1981 NFL Draft. He was named the AFC Rookie of the Year in 1981 after rushing for more than 1,100 yards. He was also selected to the Pro Bowl. "Joe was a person who was genuine and honest right to the core of his being," former Chiefs coach Marv Levy said.

No Chiefs player has worn the No. 37 jersey since Delaney's death.

Kansas City was filled with excitement going into the 1972 season. That is because the Chiefs would be opening Arrowhead Stadium that year. It was considered the best stadium in the NFL at the time. Even legendary Chicago Bears owner George Halas was impressed. He called it "the most revolutionary, futuristic sports complex I have ever seen."

More than 79,000 fans turned out for the first regular-season game at the new stadium. The Chiefs opened their season with a rematch against the Dolphins. The players tried to keep their emotions in check before such a big game.

CHIEFS LINEBACKER BOBBY BELL REACTS TO A PLAY DURING A 1971 GAME IN SAN DIEGO. BELL WAS INDUCTED INTO THE PRO FOOTBALL HALL OF FAME IN 1983.

"We can't afford to get hyped up about this game with 13 to play afterward," Chiefs running back Ed Podolak said. "What happens if you get all emotionally involved and overpeaked and then lose?"

The Chiefs did lose the game. They were beaten 20–10. They finished the year with an 8–6 record and missed the play-offs. Kansas City had another winning season in 1973 when it finished 7–5–2. But that was followed by several losing seasons.

The Chiefs began showing their age in 1974. Dawson was 39 years old and splitting time at quarterback with Mike Livingston. Several other key players were older than 30, too. They struggled to a 5–9 record that season, failing to win consecutive games for the first time in team history.

The struggles continued as the Chiefs posted 5–9 records in each of their next two seasons, as well. Dawson and star defensive tackle Buck Buchanan retired after the 1975 season. Meanwhile, the team had traded away its 1973 and 1975 first-round draft picks, making it harder to replace them.

The Chiefs hit a new low in 1977 when they finished 2–12. The team hired Marv Levy to take over as coach in 1978. Levy had been a coach in the Canadian Football League. He focused on improving the defense. The first step was taking defensive end Art Still and linebacker Gary Spani in the 1978 NFL Draft.

The Chiefs continued to struggle, however. They finished 4–12 in 1978 before finishing 7–9 in 1979. In 1980, the team released Jan Stenerud. The Chiefs struggled and lost the

THE CHIEFS DRAFTED DEFENSIVE END ART STILL IN THE 1978 NFL DRAFT.
HE SPENT 10 OF HIS 12 SEASONS IN KANSAS CITY.

first four games of the season. But behind a strong defense, the Chiefs finished the year with an 8–8 record.

That momentum carried over into the 1981 season. The Chiefs won six of their first eight games. Two of those wins were against the Oakland Raiders, the defending Super Bowl champions. But the magic soon faded. The Chiefs finished 9–7. Kansas City never won more than eight games in a season between 1982 and 1985.

The team rebounded in 1986, however. With a 24–19 win over the Pittsburgh Steelers, the Chiefs qualified for the playoffs. But their luck ran out there. They lost 35–15 to the New York Jets.

After winning eight total games over the next two seasons, the Chiefs made another change.

The Chiefs hired Carl Peterson as general manager after the 1988 season. One of his first decisions was to hire Marty Schottenheimer as the Chiefs' coach. Schottenheimer had coached the Cleveland Browns to a pair of American Football Conference (AFC) Championship Game appearances. He seemed to be the guy who could turn things around for Kansas City.

With Schottenheimer running the show, the Chiefs had new life. Linebacker Derrick Thomas was named the Defensive Rookie of the Year. Running back Christian Okoye led the NFL in rushing. Behind the efforts of those two players, the Chiefs went 8–7–1 during the 1989 season.

There was at least hope that the future was bright for Kansas City as it entered the 1990s.

DERRICK THOMAS WAS THE NFL'S DEFENSIVE ROOKIE OF THE YEAR IN 1989. HE HAD 10 SACKS AND 75 TACKLES THAT SEASON.

CHAPTER 5

SEARCHING FOR SUCCESS

Derrick Thomas helped inspire the Chiefs to succeed during the 1990 season. In a game against Seattle, Thomas sacked Seahawks quarterback Dave Krieg seven times. Although the Chiefs lost the game, 17–16, Kansas City won six of their final seven games and made the playoffs. They lost to the Miami Dolphins in the first round, however.

The Chiefs came back with a 10–6 record in 1991 but lost to the Bills in the second round of the playoffs. A 10–6 record during the 1992 regular season led to another playoff berth. After losing to the Chargers in the first round, the Chiefs decided to make a big change.

MORE THAN THE MONEY

Chiefs running back Christian Okoye was one of the league's best players in 1989, rushing for more than 1,400 yards. But his salary did not exactly match his talent. Okoye made only $215,000 that year. That was about one-seventh of what Colts running back Eric Dickerson made. That did not bother Okoye. "Being too rich can be a problem," he said. "Man does not live by money alone."

THE CHIEFS TRADED FOR QUARTERBACK JOE MONTANA, A FOUR-TIME SUPER BOWL CHAMPION, AFTER THE 1992 SEASON.

MEMORABLE MOMENT

Joe Montana was the quarterback for Kansas City in 1994. In a *Monday Night Football* game that October, he led the Chiefs into battle against legendary quarterback John Elway and the Denver Broncos.

Montana completed 34 of his 54 passes for 393 yards. He threw three touchdowns and only one interception. His 5-yard touchdown pass to Willie Davis in the final seconds gave the Chiefs a thrilling 31–28 win over the Broncos.

"Those kind of battles you get in are the fun games for a quarterback," Montana said. "You're going against the guy that can, you know if you let him back on the field, he'll do the same thing back to you."

Montana and Elway finished their respective careers as two of the best quarterbacks of all time. They won a combined six Super Bowls and were both elected into the Pro Football Hall of Fame.

The team had only won one playoff game since winning Super Bowl IV after the 1969 season. So they made a trade for Joe Montana. The star quarterback had led the San Francisco 49ers to four Super Bowl championships during the 1980s. The Chiefs also signed free agent Marcus Allen. He had been a star running back with the Los Angeles Raiders.

Montana and Allen made an impact. The Chiefs finished 11–5. They also won their first division title since 1971. Kansas City took out the Pittsburgh Steelers 27–24 in its playoff opener. The Chiefs then beat the Houston Oilers 28–20 for a berth in the AFC Championship Game. They would fall short of the Super Bowl, however. Kansas City fell to the Buffalo Bills 30–13 in the AFC Championship Game.

RUNNING BACK MARCUS ALLEN FINDS OPEN SPACE AGAINST THE RAIDERS IN 1994. HE ENTERED THE PRO FOOTBALL HALL OF FAME IN 2003.

The Chiefs came into the final game of 1994 in a must-win situation. A win against the Raiders would send Kansas City to the playoffs. A loss would end their season. Allen rushed for 133 yards against his former team, and the Chiefs won 19–9.

Their run in the playoffs did not last long, however. Kansas City lost to the Dolphins 27–17 in the first round.

In 1995, Chiefs fans had reason to believe their team might finally be good enough to return to the Super Bowl. The Chiefs had one of the best rushing offenses in the league as well as a top-notch defense. They jumped out to a 10–1 record before finishing the regular season 13–3. They then hosted the Indianapolis Colts in a chilly playoff game at Arrowhead Stadium. But Chiefs fans would again be disappointed. Kicker Lin Elliott missed three field goals in the Chiefs' 10–7 loss.

The Chiefs' run of success was over for the time being. Kansas City made the playoffs only once from 1996 to 2002. In 1997, they lost to the eventual champion Denver Broncos. After that, they failed to win more than nine games in any season—that is, until 2003.

Kansas City hired coach Dick Vermeil before the 2001 season. Vermeil had guided the St. Louis Rams to the Super Bowl XXXIV title just two years earlier. One of his first moves was trading for quarterback Trent Green. The two had worked together on the Rams. The Chiefs also added running back Priest Holmes before that season.

SACK MASTER

Derrick Thomas died from injuries suffered in an auto accident after the 1999 season. But the star linebacker will go down as an all-time great in Kansas City. The man nicknamed "D. T." was a master of sacks during the 1990s. He tallied 116.5 sacks during the decade. No other player in the NFL had more sacks in that time. He was enshrined in the Pro Football Hall of Fame in 2009.

Holmes had been undrafted out of college. So far he had been a backup in the NFL. But with the Chiefs, he exploded. In 2003,

WITH RUNNING BACK PRIEST HOLMES RUSHING FOR AN NFL-RECORD 27 TOUCHDOWNS IN 2003, THE CHIEFS STARTED THE SEASON 9–0.

he set a new NFL record with 27 touchdowns. The Chiefs were on fire, too. Behind an explosive offense, they started the season 9–0. That was a team record.

After the regular season, the Chiefs were 13–3 and the second seed in the AFC. They hosted the Indianapolis Colts in the play-offs. Both teams were known for their explosive offenses. Neither offense had to punt the ball in the game. But the Chiefs came out on the wrong end again. Indianapolis won 38–31.

It was downhill again for the Chiefs after that 2003 season. They missed the playoffs after the next two seasons, despite finishing 10–6 in 2005. Vermeil resigned after the 2005 season. The Chiefs briefly showed some signs of improvement under coach Herm Edwards. They reached the playoffs in his first season. But they again lost to the Colts in the playoffs, this time 23–8.

The Chiefs won a total of six games in 2007 and 2008. In 2009, they went 4–12 under first-year coach Todd Haley. The team's offense and defense were among the worst in the league.

More reason for hope arrived for the 2010 season. The Chiefs hired Charlie Weis as offensive coordinator and Romeo Crennel as defensive coordinator. They had both coached for the New England Patriots during their string of successful seasons.

The Chiefs are far removed from their 1960s glory days. Fans hope that the next burst of success will lead them all the way back to the Super Bowl.

CHIEFS LINEBACKER DEMORRIO WILLIAMS AMASSED 117 TACKLES IN 2009.

TIMELINE

1959	Lamar Hunt holds the first meeting to start up the American Football League after not being able to get an NFL franchise.
1960	The Dallas Texans play their first season in the AFL and finish 8–6.
1962	Dallas wins the West Division championship and defeats the Houston Oilers in the AFL Championship Game.
1963	Unable to compete with the NFL's Dallas Cowboys for fans, the Texans move to Kansas City and become the Chiefs.
1967	Kansas City wins the AFL title and plays the Green Bay Packers in Super Bowl I on January 15. The Chiefs lose 35–10.
1970	Kansas City wins the final AFL Championship Game and faces the Minnesota Vikings in Super Bowl IV. The Chiefs roll past the Vikings 23–7 on January 11.
1971	The Chiefs play their final game at Municipal Stadium against the Miami Dolphins. It is a playoff game and the Chiefs lose 27–24 in two overtimes.
1972	The Chiefs play their first season at Arrowhead Stadium. They fail to make the playoffs, however, finishing 8–6.
1974	Coach Hank Stram resigns after the season. The Chiefs finish 5–9.
1981	Kansas City goes 9–7 during the year. It is the Chiefs' first winning season since 1973.

1983	Joe Delaney, a promising running back for the Chiefs, dies while trying to save three children from drowning.
1986	Kansas City makes the playoffs for the first time in 15 years. The Chiefs lose their playoff opener 35–15 to the New York Jets.
1989	Marty Schottenheimer is hired after a 4–11–1 season. He is a former coach of the Cleveland Browns.
1989	Derrick Thomas is drafted out of Alabama and wins the Defensive Rookie of the Year Award.
1993	The Chiefs bring in NFL greats Joe Montana and Marcus Allen. The team wins the Western Division for the first time since 1971 but is eliminated by Buffalo in the playoffs.
1994	Joe Montana and Marcus Allen help lead the Chiefs to the playoffs again. Kansas City goes down to Miami 27–17.
1995	Kansas City finishes 13–3 and is a favorite to win the Super Bowl. The dream ends in a 10–7 loss to the Indianapolis Colts in the playoffs.
2003	The Chiefs go 13–3 in the regular season and win the AFC West title. Their success ends in a 38–31 loss to the Indianapolis Colts in the playoffs.
2006	Chiefs owner Lamar Hunt dies at age 74. The Chiefs make the playoffs but lose 23–8 to the Indianapolis Colts.
2009	The Chiefs finish 4–12, but in the offseason the franchise hires offensive coordinator Charlie Weis and defensive coordinator Romeo Crennel.

QUICK STATS

FRANCHISE HISTORY

Dallas Texans (AFL) 1960–62
Kansas City Chiefs (AFL and NFL)
    1963–

SUPER BOWLS
(wins in bold)

1966 (I), **1969 (IV)**

AFL CHAMPIONSHIPS
(1960–69; wins in bold)

1962, 1966, 1969

AFC CHAMPIONSHIP GAMES
(since 1970 AFL-NFL merger)

1993

DIVISION CHAMPIONSHIPS
(since 1970 AFL-NFL merger)

1971, 1993, 1995, 1997, 2003

KEY PLAYERS
(position, seasons with team)

Marcus Allen (RB, 1993–97)
Bobby Bell (DE-LB, 1963–74)
Buck Buchanan (DT, 1963–75)
Len Dawson (QB, 1962–75)
Abner Haynes (HB, 1960–64)
Priest Holmes (RB, 2001–07)
Willie Lanier (LB, 1967–77)
Joe Montana (QB, 1993–94)
Ed Podolak (RB, 1969–77)
Gary Spani (LB, 1978–86)
Jan Stenerud (K, 1967–79)
Art Still (DE, 1978–87)
Otis Taylor (WR, 1965–75)
Derrick Thomas (LB, 1989–1999)
Emmitt Thomas (CB, 1966–78)

KEY COACHES

Marty Schottenheimer (1989–98):
    101–58–1; 3–7 (playoffs)
Hank Stram (1960–74): 124–76–10;
    5–3 (playoffs)

HOME FIELDS

Arrowhead Stadium (1972–)
Kansas City Municipal Stadium
    (1963–71)
Cotton Bowl (1960–62)

* All statistics through 2009 season

QUOTES AND ANECDOTES

Many people believed the American Football League was a bad idea. As such, they nicknamed the eight founding owners in the league the "Foolish Club." Dallas Texans owner Lamar Hunt was among those owners. The league played a 14-game schedule. Every team played the others twice. It turned out to be a good thing for fans. They were given an opportunity to see every team in the league each year.

"It was really tough because there is no question that I had a lot to do with losing the game," Jan Stenerud said about his poor performance in the 1971 playoffs against Miami. "It was hard to take, but time, I guess, heals everything. The only thing I can do is try to block out the memory of what happened, but I probably will think about it all this week, and during the game, too."

Kansas City's Dante Hall tied an NFL record with his sixth career kickoff-return touchdown in an October 2005 game against the Philadelphia Eagles. His return went for 96 yards in the second quarter of a 37–31 loss. The kickoff return for a touchdown was the tenth total kick return touchdown of his career (six kickoff returns and four punt returns). He returned kicks for touchdowns in four straight games in 2003.

Former Kansas City running back Christian Okoye once punished defenses with his hard running ability. He now helps young boys and girls through his foundation. He enjoys being a role model. "Anytime a person succeeds, whether you like it or not, you are a role model," Okoye said. "Whether I like it or not, it is the case. I like it. I chose to embrace it."

GLOSSARY

attendance

The number of fans at a game or the total number of fans attending games in a season.

blitz

To charge directly and immediately at the passer.

clinch

To officially settle something, such as a berth in the playoffs.

contend

To compete.

draft

A system used by professional sports leagues to select new players in order to spread incoming talent among all teams.

franchise player

An athlete who is not simply the best player on their team, but one a team builds around for the foreseeable future.

legendary

Well-known and admired over a long period of time.

merger

Combining together.

retire

To officially end one's career.

rival

An opponent that brings out great emotion in a team, its fans, and its players.

rookie

A first-year professional athlete.

ticket broker

A person who purchases tickets to an event and then re-sells them.

FOR MORE INFORMATION

Further Reading

Flanagan, Jeffrey, and The Kansas City Star. *A Sea of Red: 50 Years With the Chiefs and The Kansas City Star*. Kansas City, MO: Kansas City Star Books, 2009.

MacCambridge, Michael. *America's Game: The Epic Story of How Pro Football Captured a Nation*. New York: Random House, 2004.

Sports Illustrated. *The Football Book Expanded Edition*. New York: Sports Illustrated Books, 2009.

Web Links

To learn more about the Kansas City Chiefs, visit ABDO Publishing Company online at **www.abdopublishing.com**. Web sites about the Chiefs are featured on our Book Links page. These links are routinely monitored and updated to provide the most current information available.

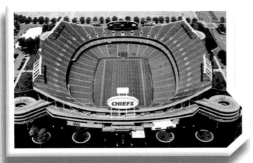

Places to Visit

Arrowhead Stadium
One Arrowhead Drive
Kansas City, MO 64129
816-920-9400
http://www.kcchiefs.com/arrowhead/index.html
The Kansas City Chiefs home stadium since 1972.

Kansas City Chiefs Headquarters
One Arrowhead Drive
Kansas City, MO 64129
816-920-9300
http://www.kcchiefs.com
The team's headquarters and practice facility are here. In July and August, the team holds its training camp here as well. Some of those practices are open to the public.

Pro Football Hall of Fame
2121 George Halas Dr., NW
Canton, OH 44708
330-456-8207
www.profootballhof.com
This hall of fame and museum highlights the greatest players and moments in the history of the National Football League. Fourteen people affiliated with the Chiefs are enshrined, including Len Dawson, Lamar Hunt, and Derrick Thomas.

INDEX

About the Author

Brian Lester is a sports writer in Findlay, Ohio, where he lives with his wife and daughter. He has covered athletics at every level, from high school to the pros, and has spent the last eight years covering the University of Findlay for *The Courier* in Findlay. He was named the best sports writer in Virginia in the nondaily newspaper category in 1998 and has won two Associated Press Awards in Ohio.